THE PHYSICIAN
LESSONS ON CHRISTIAN HEALTH

THE NAMES OF CHRIST ILLUSTRATRED
ACTIVITY BOOK

THE NOC ILLUSTRATED ACTIVITY BOOKS: AN AMAZING WAY TO TEACH YOUTH THE MANY DIFFERENT CHARACTERS OF CHRIST FOUND IN THE HOLY SCRIPTURES.

ISBN: 1-441-46166-3

PRINTED IN THE UNITED STATES OF AMERICA

COVER PAGE DESIGNED BY DYNAMIC ANIMATION PRODUCTIONS, LLC

PREFACE

"WHEN JESUS HEARD IT, HE SAITH UNTO THEM, THEY THAT ARE WHOLE HAVE NO NEED OF THE PHYSICIAN, BUT THEY THAT ARE SICK: I CAME NOT TO CALL THE RIGHTEOUS, BUT SINNERS TO REPENTANCE." MARK 2:17 (KJV)

TO OUR PARENTS, TEACHERS AND GUARDIANS: IT IS A PRIVILEGE TO STUDY GOD'S WORD WITH YOUR CHILDREN AND A BLESSING TO TRAIN AND DISCIPLINE THEM FOR SERVICE IN THE MASTER'S CAUSE. ALONG WITH THEIR BIBLES, WE STRONGLY ENCOURAGE YOUR PARTICIPATION IN THE CHILD'S USAGE OF THIS ACTIVITY BOOK.

LESSONS ON HEALTH: 8 LAWS
CROSSWORD PUZZLE 1

ACROSS

4. PHYSICAL OR MENTAL STRENGTH, ENERGY, OR FORCE.

6. FIRM RELIANCE ON THE INTEGRITY, ABILITY, OR CHARACTER OF A PERSON OR THING. BELIEVE IN.

7. MODERATION; SELF-RESTRAINT; HABITUAL MODERATION IN REGARD TO THE INDULGENCE OF THE NATURAL APPETITES AND ZEAL.

9. TO MOLD OR MAKE INTO A PARTICULAR FORM; TO GIVE FORM OR FIGURE TO.

10. THE FLUID WE BREATH.

11. EXERTION OF THE BODY, AS CONDUCIVE TO HEALTH; ACTION.

12. SUITABLENESS; ADAPTATION; PREPARATION QUALIFIED FOR.

DOWN

1. A CONDITION PROMOTING SANITARY PRACTICES. PROMOTION AND PRESERVATION OF HEALTH.

2. QUIET RELAXATION; REPOSE, A STATE FREE FROM MOTION OR DISTURBANCE; SLEEP.

3. A FLUID. THE MOST ABUNDANT AND MOST NECESSARY FOR LIVING BEINGS OF ANY IN NATURE, EXCEPT AIR.

5. THE LIGHT FROM THE BIGGEST STAR IN THE SOLAR SYSTEM; THE DIRECT RAYS OF IT.

8. THAT WHICH NOURISHES; NUTRIMENT; THE ACT OR PROCESS OF PROMOTING THE GROWTH OR REPAIRING.

9. FIRMNESS; SOLIDITY OR TOUGHNESS; THE POWER TO RESIST ATTACK.

CROSSWORD PUZZLE 1: ANSWERS FOUND ON PAGE 36

FILL IN THE BLANK
COMMIT THESE VERSES OF SCRIPTURE TO MEMORY

JESUS _____ AND SAID UNTO HER, _____ DRINKETH OF THIS _____ SHALL _____ AGAIN: BUT WHOSOEVER _____ OF THE WATER THAT I SHALL GIVE HIM SHALL _____ THIRST; BUT THE WATER THAT I SHALL GIVE HIM SHALL BE IN HIM A _____ OF WATER _____ UP INTO _____ LIFE. ~ JOHN 4:13

LET YOUR _____ BE KNOWN UNTO _____ MEN. THE _____ IS AT HAND. ~ PHILIPPIANS 4:5

AND _____, BY THESE, MY SON, BE _____: OF _____ MANY _____ THERE IS NO END; AND MUCH _____ IS A _____ OF THE _____. ~ ECCLESIASTES 12:12

_____ UNTO ME, ALL YE THAT _____ AND ARE HEAVY _____, AND I WILL _____ YOU _____. ~ MATTHEW 11:28

WHETHER THEREFORE YE _____, OR _____, OR WHATSOEVER YE _____, DO ALL TO THE _____ OF GOD. ~ 1 CORINTHIANS 10:31

SEE HOW MANY WORDS
YOU CAN MAKE OUT OF
RESTING

"AND ON THE SEVENTH DAY GOD ENDED HIS WORK WHICH HE HAD MADE;
AND HE RESTED ON THE SEVENTH DAY FROM ALL HIS WORK WHICH HE HAD MADE." ~ GENESIS 2:2

_____

_____

_____

_____   _____

_____   _____

_____   _____

_____   _____

COLORING ACTIVITY

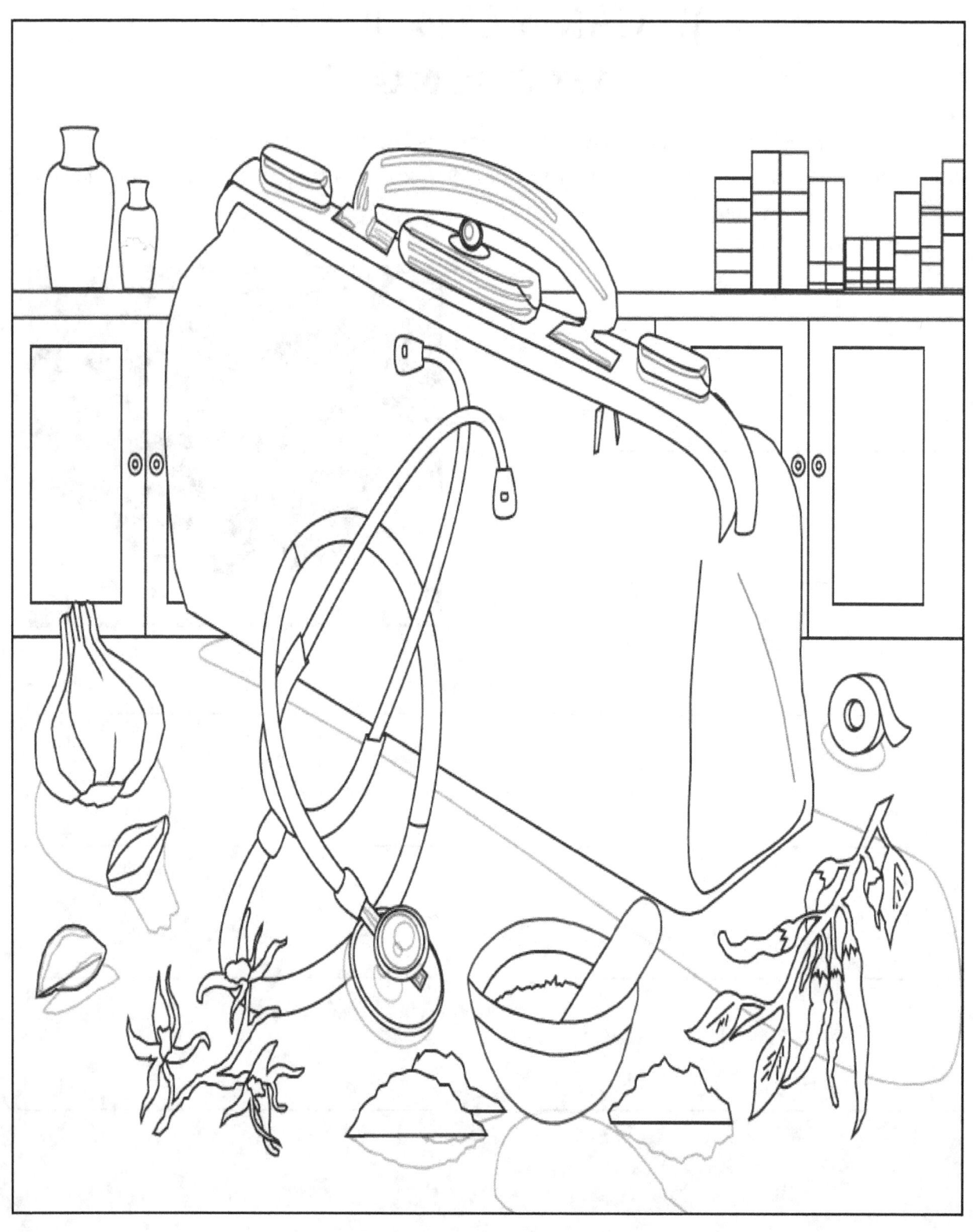

THE PHYSICIAN

SECRET MESSAGE 1

A	B	C	D	E	F	G	H	I	J	K	L	M	N	O	P	Q	R	S	T	U	V	W	X	Y	Z
9	4	15	21	26	10	18	5	16	1	13	6	23	8	2	14	24	11	3	17	25	7	19	12	20	22

USE THE ABOVE KEYS TO DECODE THE MESSAGE BELOW

— — — — —   — —   — — — —   — — — — — — — —
17 5 26 11 26   16 3   17 5 9 17   3 14 26 9 13 26 17 5

— — — —   — — —   — — — — — — — — —   — —
6 16 13 26   17 5 26   14 16 26 11 15 16 8 18 3   2 10

— — — — — —   — — —   — — —   — — — — — —
9 3 19 2 11 21   4 25 17   17 5 26   17 2 8 18 25 26

— —   — — —   — — — —   — —   — — — — — —
2 10   17 5 26   19 16 3 26   16 3   5 26 9 6 17 5

WHERE IS THIS TEXT FOUND? _____

SECRET MESSAGE 1: ANSWERS FOUND ON PAGE 34

BIBLE TRIVIA 1: FOOD FOR THOUGHT

1. WHO WAS A FAMOUS EATER OF LOCUSTS? (MATTHEW 3:4)

2. WHAT FOUR YOUNG MEN REFUSED TO EAT THE RICH FOODS OF A KING? (DANIEL 1:5-8)

3. WHO TRADED HIS BREAD AND LENTILS FOR HIS BROTHER'S BIRTHRIGHT? (GENESIS 25:31-34)

4. WHO HAD A BAKER WHO MADE PASTRIES FOR HIM? (GENESIS 40:1-5)

5. WHAT INCIDENT IN DAVID'S LIFE CAUSED PEOPLE TO BRING HIM ALL MANNER OF FOODS TO EAT? (1 SAMUEL 25:1-18)

6. ACCORDING TO THE LAW, WHAT FOODS COMPOSED THE PASSOVER MEAL? (EXODUS 12:8-11)

7. WHAT OLD MAN WAS DECEIVED WHEN HIS SON, DRESSED IN GOATSKIN, PRESENTED HIM WITH A MEAL OF COOKED GOAT? (GENESIS 27:19-24)

8. WHAT DID EZEKIEL'S EDIBLE SCROLL TASTE LIKE IN HIS MOUTH? (EZEKIEL 3:1-3)

9. WHAT JUDGE OF ISRAEL COOKED AN ANGEL A MEAL THAT INCLUDED A POT OF BROTH? (JUDGES 6:19-21)

10. IN WHAT BOOK OF THE BIBLE IS CANAAN FIRST DESCRIBED AS A LAND FLOWING WITH MILK AND HONEY?

BIBLE TRIVIA 1: ANSWERS FOUND ON PAGE 32

SEE HOW MANY WORDS
YOU CAN MAKE OUT OF
TEMPERANCE

"LET YOUR MODERATION BE KNOWN UNTO ALL MEN. THE LORD IS AT HAND." ~ PHILIPPIANS 4:5

_____

_____

_____

_____   _____

_____   _____

_____   _____

_____   _____

LESSONS ON HEALTH

FIND THESE WORDS IN THE FOREST OF LETTERS

```
U O Z Y G E E V V U S U B P V C A D V P V Y L N D
D S R O C N U Z F O R W M E X E R C I S E P U Y H
I F H I E M V G B S R O G S A N E I A F E R N E A
S N X I Z U E A I M W T X R O N B R U L T G B E O
A I G W J L B C W I I W I I C L T T V W Y P H O H
C Y D P E W A T E R Y W T E J L P Y B U M K H Y P
H T F N O K T H E R K I Z W V W Y I M M I B X F S
P Q J C E H J T I L R L C G Y E I C T R S C V L H
J E W P J E B A E T I V P K C Q V S R K O F E C A
M S G E P Q H W U X B Q Y P W N C W T M Y Z L T P
M N U J O O S N M V I G O R I W T A I R W S S P E
E P G N B E K A W X M Y Y W U U K G E V E U R B P
C K Q W L U F X R T E M P E R A N C E S R N Z G Q
D X H Q R I X R C E E A E O S I K G X T G N G K C
X B S P M K G A V T S T F I T N E S S M J O D T S
J B L F L M N H V W A T N C V Z T A X G S F X U H
F O P C J O B I T A Z E V F F E D I Q N X D C S V
```

NUTRITION	EXERCISE	WATER	SUNLIGHT
TEMPERANCE	AIR	REST	TRUST
HYGIENE	FITNESS	STRENGTH	VIGOR
SHAPE			

WORD SEARCH 1: ANSWERS FOUND ON PAGE 37

"FINDING HEALTH IS KEY IN THE WORD OF GOD"

SEEK AND FIND YOUR WAY THROUGH THE MAZE BELOW

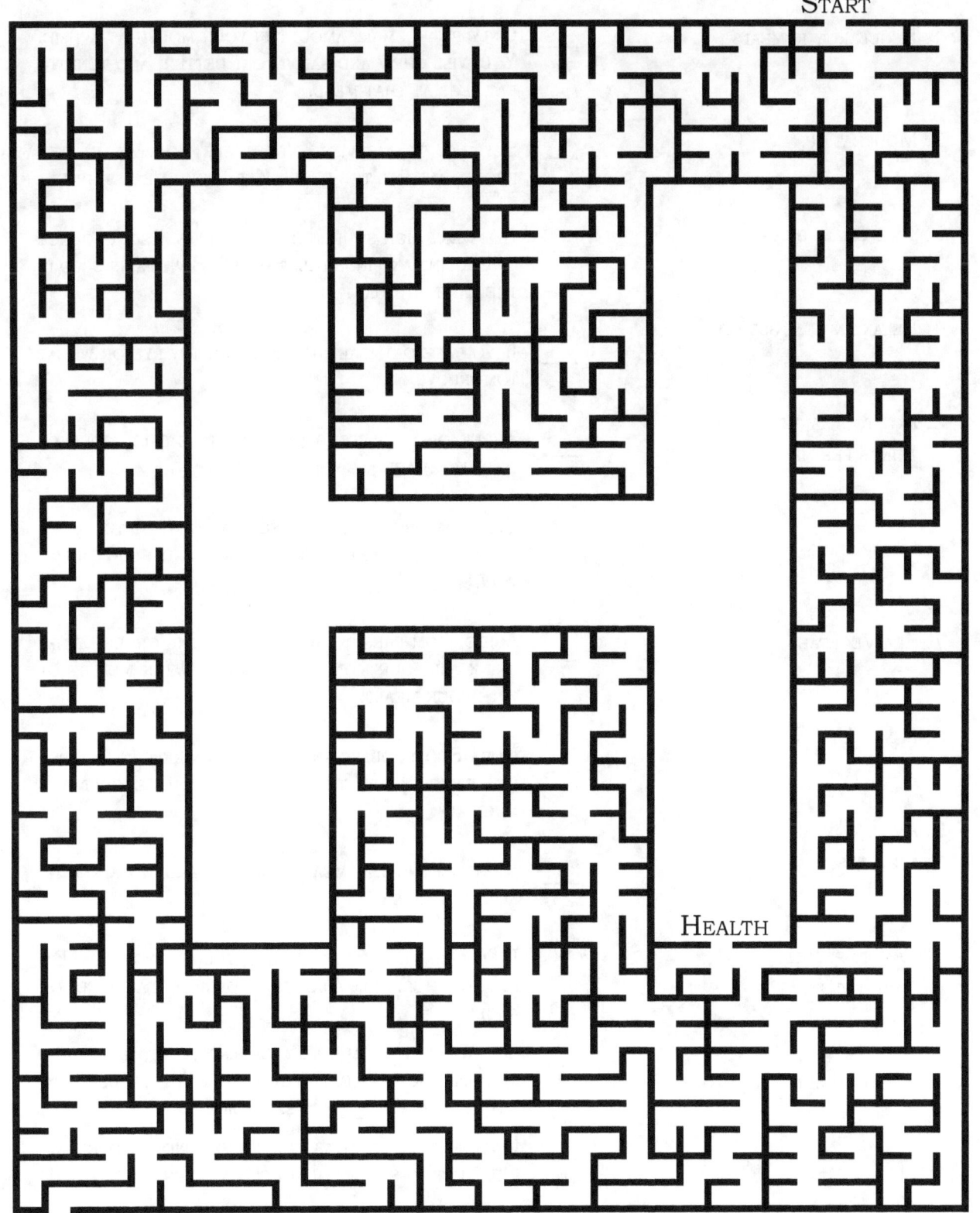

START

HEALTH

9

CONCEPTS ON HEALTH: BASIC PRINCIPLES 1
WRITE THE NUMBER NEXT TO ITS MATCHING DEFINITION

1. REGULARITY IN MEALS

2. MODERATION

3. TAKE SMALL BITES

4. RELAX AND EAT SLOWLY

5. NOT TOO MANY
   THINGS PER MEAL

6. NO DRINKING

7. SEA VEGETABLE

8. MIXED UP

9. AVOID COMPLICATED
   MIXTURES

10. AVOID PECULIAR
    ADDITIVES

11. VARY YOUR MEALS

12. BLACK STRAP

____ ONLY PUT A SMALL AMOUNT IN YOUR MOUTH AT A TIME. YOU WILL CHEW AND SALIVATE IT BETTER, AND TEND TO EAT LESS AT THAT MEAL.

____ SAY NO TO GRAVIES, VEGETABLE LOAVES, GLUTEN FOODS, AND ALL THE REST. KEEP YOUR MEAL SIMPLE.

____ IT IS VERY RICH SOURCE OF IRON. IT IS ALSO A SOURCE OF CHOLINE AND INOSITOL, THE TWO B VITAMINS USED IN THE LARGEST QUANTITIES.

____ IF YOU ATE OATMEAL THIS MORNING, TRY RYE OR WHEAT TOMORROW.

____ THREE OR FOUR ITEMS (PLUS A LITTLE SALT, CORRECT OILS, ETC.) ARE ALL YOU NEED.

____ SUCH AS VINEGAR, MONOSODIUM GLUTAMATE, ETC., WHICH ONLY UPSET YOUR STOMACH AND SLOW DIGESTION.

____ ASIDE FROM FRESH, RAW JUICES OR THE GREEN DRINK, DRINK ALL YOUR LIQUIDS (WATER) BETWEEN MEALS NOT WITH YOUR MEALS.

____ NOVA SCOTIA DULSE AND NORWEGIAN KELP (TWO TYPES OF SEAWEED) ARE THE ONLY RICH SOURCE OF TRACE MINERALS.

____ REST BEFORE THE MEAL AND WALK AROUND AFTER IT, NOT VICE VERSA.

____ IF YOU ARE TOO RUSHED TO EAT, THEN DO NOT EAT. DO NOT BE HURRIED, ANXIOUS, WORRIED, FATIGUED OR ANGRY.

____ DO NOT EAT THEM EARLY OR LATE, BUT MAINTAIN A REGULAR SCHEDULE. YOUR STOMACH IS USED TO EATING AT CERTAIN TIMES EACH DAY.

____ ONLY EAT AS MUCH AS YOU NEED. NEVER OVEREAT. ONLY EAT TO SATISFY HUNGER, AND THEN STOP.

DEFINITIONS: ANSWERS FOUND ON PAGE 35

SECRET MESSAGE 2

A	B	C	D	E	F	G	H	I	J	K	L	M	N	O	P	Q	R	S	T	U	V	W	X	Y	Z
24	8	16	1	15	26	10	3	17	4	13	23	14	7	18	22	6	19	12	25	11	20	2	9	21	5

USE THE ABOVE KEYS TO DECODE THE MESSAGE BELOW

A N D   I S A I A H   S A I D ,
24 7 1   17 12 24 17 24 3   12 24 17 1 ,

T A K E   A
25 24 13 15   24

L U M P   O F   F I G S .
23 11 14 22   18 26   26 17 10 12 .

A N D   T H E Y
24 7 1   25 3 15 21

T O O K   A N D   L A I D   I T   O N   T H E
25 18 18 13   24 7 1   23 24 17 1   17 25   18 7   25 3 15

B O I L ,   A N D   H E   R E C O V E R E D .
8 18 17 23 ,   24 7 1   3 15   19 15 16 18 20 15 19 15 1 .

WHERE IS THIS TEXT FOUND? _____

SECRET MESSAGE 2: ANSWERS FOUND ON PAGE 34

LESSONS ON HEALTH: ESSENTIAL OILS
CROSSWORD PUZZLE 2

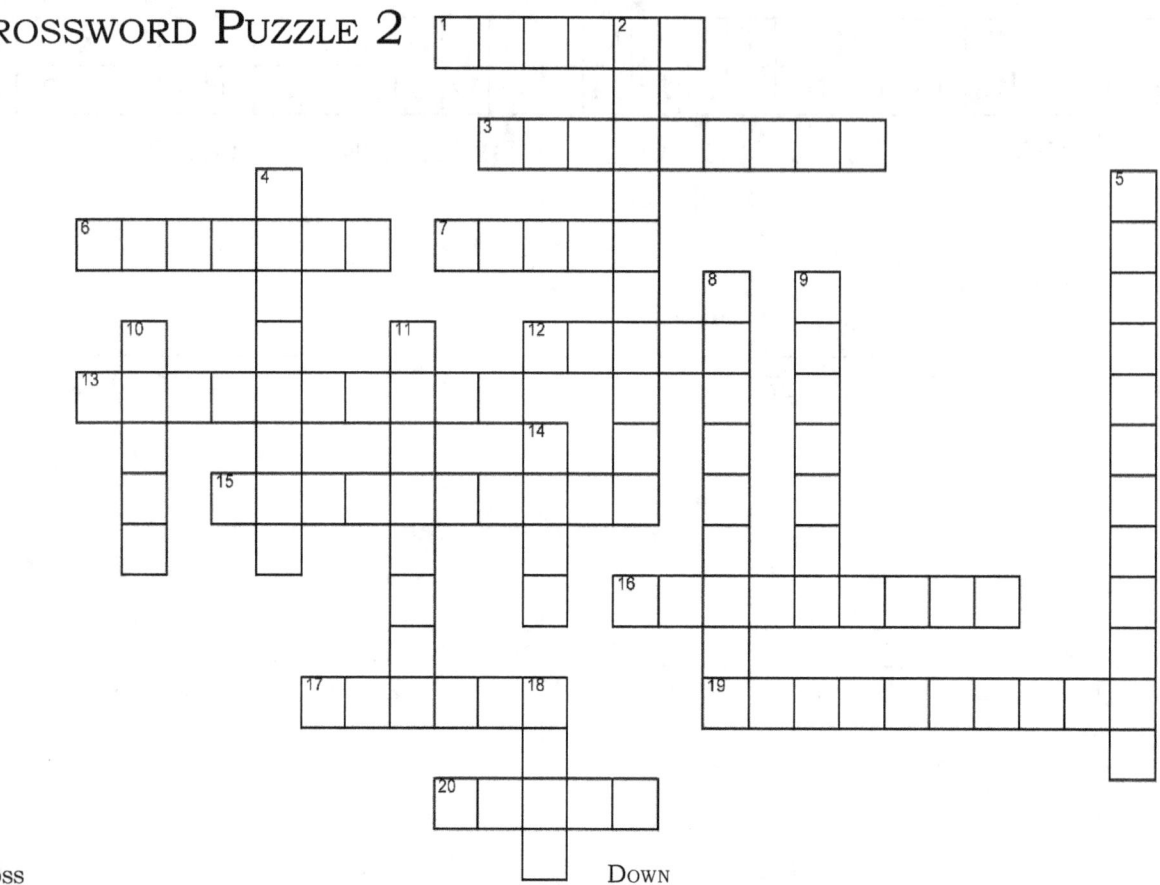

ACROSS

1. EVERGREEN TREES IN WARM REGIONS WITH A YELLOWISH OR REDDISH RIND AND A SECTIONED, PULPY INTERIOR.

3. AN AROMATIC EURASIAN PLANT HAVING CLUSTERS OF SMALL PURPLISH FLOWERS AND YIELDING AN OIL USED WIDELY AS A FLAVORING. A SPECIES OF MINT.

6. AN HERB OF THE MINT FAMILY USED IN TOMATO SAUCES AND PIZZA.

7. EVERGREEN TREE IN WARM REGIONS FOR ITS AROMATIC DRIED FLOWER BUDS WHICH ARE USED WHOLE OR GROUND AS A SPICE.

12. AN AROMATIC GUM RESIN OBTAINED FROM SEVERAL TREES AND SHRUBS OF INDIA, ARABIA, AND EASTERN AFRICA, USED IN PERFUME AND INCENSE. ALSO CALLED BALM OF GILEAD.

13. A TROPICAL GRASS NATIVE TO SOUTHERN INDIA AND SRI LANKA, YIELDING AN AROMATIC OIL USED AS FLAVORING AND MEDICINE.

15. A PLANT, MENTHA PIPERITA, HAVING SMALL PURPLE OR WHITE FLOWERS AND DOWNY LEAVES THAT YIELD A PUNGENT OIL.

16. A PLANT OF THE GENUS NARDUS. USED IN THE ANOINTING OF JESUS' FEET BEFORE THE LAST SUPPER.

17. A PLANT OF TROPICAL ASIA WITH JOINTED ROOTS AND STALKS THAT RISE TWO OR THREE FEET WITH NARROW LEAVES.

19. NATIVE TO AUSTRALIA, HAVING AROMATIC LEAVES THAT YIELD AN OIL USED MEDICINALLY AND WOOD VALUED AS TIMBER.

20. AN OLD WORLD AROMATIC ANNUAL HERB IN THE MINT FAMILY, CULTIVATED FOR ITS LEAVES WHICH ARE USED AS A SEASONING.

DOWN

2. A LARGE, ROUNDISH, YELLOW-SKINNED EDIBLE CITRUS FRUIT HAVING A JUICY, ACID PULP.

4. USED AS AN AID TO SLEEP, RELAXATION, SOOTHING HEADACHES AND HEALING INSECT BITES. PALE PURPLE TO PALE VIOLET.

5. USED FOR ANOINTING AND WAS GIVEN TO THE CHILD JESUS AS A GIFT.

8. USED IN TEAS TO AID WITH SLEEP AND DIGESTION. GIVES A CALMING EFFECT.

9. ANY OF NUMEROUS SHRUBS OR VINES BELONGING TO THE OLIVE FAMILY USED IN PERFUMERY.

10. A SPINY, EVERGREEN TREE WIDELY CULTIVATED FOR ITS YELLOW, EGG-SHAPED FRUIT WITH COOLING ACID JUICE.

11. A PLANT USED AS A REMEDY FOR INSOMNIA WITH FRAGRANT WHITE TO PINK OR LAVENDER FLOWERS.

14. A SPECIES OF ACID FRUIT, GREEN AND SMALLER THAN THE LEMON.

18. A FLOWER HAVING PRICKLY STEMS, COMPOUND LEAVES, AND VARIOUSLY COLORED, OFTEN FRAGRANT FLOWERS.

CROSSWORD PUZZLE 2: ANSWERS FOUND ON PAGE 36

SEE HOW MANY WORDS
YOU CAN MAKE OUT OF
SUNSHINE

"TRULY THE LIGHT IS SWEET, AND A PLEASANT THING IT IS FOR THE EYES TO BEHOLD THE SUN."
~ ECCLESIASTES 11:7

_____

_____

_____

_____   _____

_____   _____

_____   _____

_____   _____

BIBLE TRIVIA 2: FOOD FOR THOUGHT

1. WHAT PRIZED ANIMAL WAS KILLED FOR FOOD WHEN THE PRODIGAL SON RETURNED HOME? (LUKE 15:20-24)

2. IN WHAT COUNTRY DID THE HEBREWS FEED ON CUCUMBERS, MELONS, LEEKS, ONIONS, AND GARLIC? (NUMBERS 11:5)

3. WHEN JACOB'S SONS MADE A SECOND TRIP TO EGYPT, WHAT FOODS DID THEY BRING WITH THEM AS A GIFT FOR JOSEPH? (GENESIS 43:11)

4. WHAT PROPHET, WHO WAS A HERDSMAN AND FRUIT PICKER BY TRADE, HAD A VISION OF A BASKET OF RIPE FRUIT? (AMOS 8:1-2)

5. WHO ATE HONEY OUT OF A LION'S CARCASS? (JUDGES 14:5-9)

6. WHAT MIRACULOUS FOOD RESEMBLED CORIANDER SEED? (EXODUS 16:31)

7. WHAT FOOD DID JESUS SAY IS NOT ENOUGH FOR MEN TO LIVE BY? (MATTHEW 4:4)

8. WHO FED ELIJAH CAKE, BAKED ON COALS, THAT GAVE HIM STRENGTH FOR FORTY DAYS AND FORTY NIGHTS? (1 KINGS 19:5-8)

9. WHO HAD THE PRIVILEGE OF MULTIPLYING A HANDFUL OF MEAL AND A CRUSE OF OIL? (1 KINGS 17:11-14)

BIBLE TRIVIA 2: ANSWERS FOUND ON PAGE 32

ESSENTIAL OILS

FIND THESE WORDS IN THE FOREST OF LETTERS

```
U G Z Q C I O O Z B B F D L C D N L F E Y R Q N I
G I V W A W L L B R T A Q P X E Y I N I Y W F O W D
A D T A A S E T N E B I I U U Y Y G S M X G K S U
W X F E L N P I K A G U L K C V A A B Q E R A W E
T U K F I E M I X E Q A T W A P Y C L L K A S K F
P O U M R R R Z K L M K N R L N O H S S W P P S T
Q C S W E A B I O E Y Y U O Y F U A W X I E E V E
U A C P T L N F A L N M R Q P J A M H O O F A N J
J S P L T J E K W N E A Y J T C F O C N G R R O I
K E R O O H W M I Q C M R A U Z G M L T Y U M C C
P O J R R V G Q O N M N O D S E D I A Q O I I T V
U V N A L B E O C N C X Z N J S B L V S H T N M H
M B S N X Q B I S K G E X S J E B E E Q Y Q T M P
U A K G P D U Z B Q Y R N A B J P R N E P O P Y G
V S L E L A A K L E O T A S M L A O D W U L N R Y
T I R D G I N G E R Z L Y S E X N G E X P N S R C
L L D D P A O E U U D H L S S G H Y R V G T E H R
```

LEMON	PEPPERMINT	CLOVE	FRANKINCENSE
LAVENDER	LIME	MYRRH	ORANGE
OREGANO	ROSE	SPEARMINT	SPIKENARD
VALERIAN	BASIL	CHAMOMILE	EUCALYPTUS
GINGER	GRAPEFRUIT	JASMINE	LEMONGRASS

WORD SEARCH 2: ANSWERS FOUND ON PAGE 37

SECRET MESSAGE 3

A	B	C	D	E	F	G	H	I	J	K	L	M	N	O	P	Q	R	S	T	U	V	W	X	Y	Z
17	6	20	2	21	24	13	4	14	8	22	1	26	7	18	25	9	3	15	23	5	16	10	19	11	12

USE THE ABOVE KEYS TO DECODE THE MESSAGE BELOW

"AND SAID, IF THOU WILT DILIGENTLY HEARKEN TO THE VOICE OF THE LORD THY GOD, AND WILT DO THAT WHICH IS RIGHT IN HIS SIGHT, AND WILT GIVE EAR TO HIS COMMANDMENTS, AND KEEP ALL HIS STATUTES, I WILL PUT NONE OF THESE DISEASES UPON THEE, WHICH I HAVE BROUGHT UPON THE EGYPTIANS: FOR I AM THE LORD THAT HEALETH THEE."

___ ___ ___ ___ ___ ___   ___ : ___
21 19 18   2   5 15   S   M

"AND THE LORD WILL TAKE AWAY FROM THEE ALL SICKNESS, AND WILL PUT NONE OF THE EVIL DISEASES OF EGYPT, WHICH THOU KNOWEST, UPON THEE; BUT WILL LAY THEM UPON ALL THEM THAT HATE THEE."

___ ___ ___ ___ ___ ___ ___ ___ ___ ___ ___   ___ : ___
 2 21   5 23 21   3 18   7 18 26 11   N   S

"WITH LONG LIFE WILL I SATISFY HIM, AND SHEW HIM MY SALVATION."

___ ___ ___ ___ ___ ___   ___ ___ : ___
25 15 17   1 26 15   Q   L   V

"FOR I WILL RESTORE HEALTH UNTO THEE, AND I WILL HEAL THEE OF THY WOUNDS, SAITH THE LORD; BECAUSE THEY CALLED THEE AN OUTCAST, SAYING, THIS IS ZION, WHOM NO MAN SEEKETH AFTER."

___ ___ ___ ___ ___ ___ ___ ___   ___ 0 : ___
 8 21   3 21 26 14 17   4   R   ~   A

"SURELY HE HATH BORNE OUR GRIEFS, AND CARRIED OUR SORROWS: YET WE DID ESTEEM HIM STRICKEN, SMITTEN OF GOD, AND AFFLICTED. BUT HE WAS WOUNDED FOR OUR TRANSGRESSIONS, HE WAS BRUISED FOR OUR INIQUITIES: THE CHASTISEMENT OF OUR PEACE WAS UPON HIM; AND WITH HIS STRIPES WE ARE HEALED."

___ ___ ___ ___ ___ ___   ___ ___ : ___ -
14 15 17 14 17   4   U   R   H   U

SECRET MESSAGE 3: ANSWERS FOUND ON PAGE 34

SEE HOW MANY WORDS
YOU CAN MAKE OUT OF
NUTRITION

"AND GOD SAID, BEHOLD, I HAVE GIVEN YOU EVERY HERB BEARING SEED, WHICH IS UPON THE FACE OF ALL THE EARTH, AND EVERY TREE, IN THE WHICH IS THE FRUIT OF A TREE YIELDING SEED; TO YOU IT SHALL BE FOR MEAT." ~ GENESIS 1:29

_____

_____

_____

_____   _____

_____   _____

_____   _____

_____   _____

LESSONS ON HEALTH: TYPES OF POULTICES
CROSSWORD PUZZLE 3

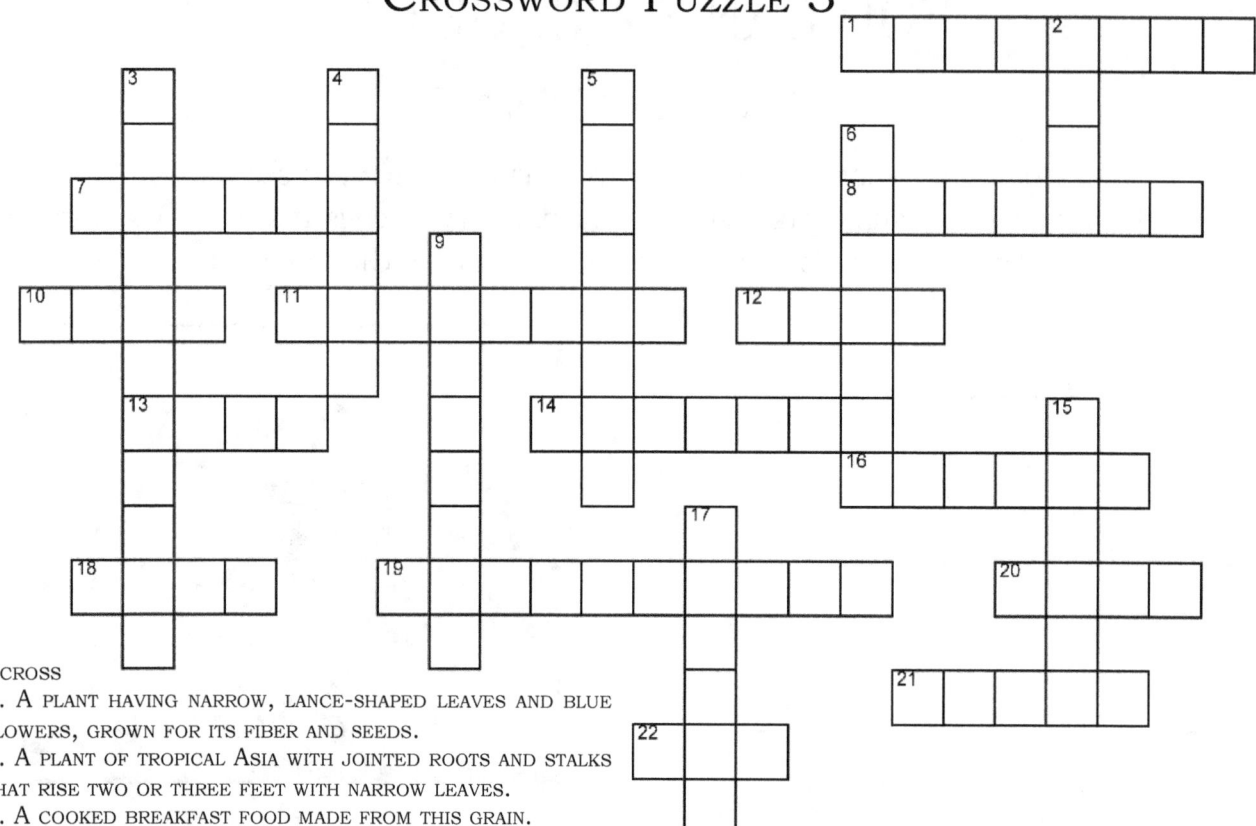

ACROSS

1. A PLANT HAVING NARROW, LANCE-SHAPED LEAVES AND BLUE FLOWERS, GROWN FOR ITS FIBER AND SEEDS.

7. A PLANT OF TROPICAL ASIA WITH JOINTED ROOTS AND STALKS THAT RISE TWO OR THREE FEET WITH NARROW LEAVES.

8. A COOKED BREAKFAST FOOD MADE FROM THIS GRAIN.

10. THE DRIED RIPE CONES OF THE FEMALE FLOWERS OF THIS PLANT ARE USED IN BREWING AND MEDICINE.

11. A SOFT MOIST MASS OF BREAD, MEAL, CLAY, OR OTHER ADHESIVE SUBSTANCE, USUALLY HEATED, TO WARM, MOISTEN, OR STIMULATE AN INFLAMED PART OF THE BODY.

12. A PROTEIN-RICH FOOD COAGULATED FROM AN EXTRACT OF SOYBEANS AND USED IN SALADS AND VARIOUS COOKED FOODS.

13. A CEREAL GRASS, ORYZA SATIVA, WHICH IS CULTIVATED EXTENSIVELY IN WARM CLIMATES FOR ITS EDIBLE GRAIN.

14. PART OF THE MUSTARD FAMILY WITH A SHORT STEM AND LEAVES FORMED INTO A EDIBLE HEAD THAT CAN BE EATEN COOKED OR RAW.

16. A COMPOSITE PLANT HAVING FERNLIKE LEAVES AND FLAT-TOPPED CLUSTERS OF WHITISH OR YELLOW FLOWERS.

18. A NATURAL EARTHY MATERIAL THAT IS PLASTIC WHEN WET, CONSISTING ESSENTIALLY OF HYDRATED SILICATES OF ALUMINUM.

19. AN ALCOHOLIC SOLUTION CONTAINING AN EXTRACT OF THE BARK AND LEAVES OF THIS PLANT IS APPLIED EXTERNALLY AS AN ASTRINGENT.

20. A CRYSTALLINE SOLID, USED EXTENSIVELY IN GROUND OR GRANULATED FORM AS A FOOD SEASONING AND PRESERVATIVE. AN ELEMENT OF SEAWATER.

21. A PLANT WITH ROUNDED EDIBLE BULBS COMPOSED OF FLESHY, TIGHT, CONCENTRIC LEAF BASES HAVING A PUNGENT ODOR AND TASTE.

22. A TREE OR SHRUB OF THE MULBERRY FAMILY BEARING A PEAR-SHAPED FRUIT THAT IS EATEN FRESH, PRESERVED, OR DRIED.

DOWN

2. A PLANT OF THE MINT FAMILY WHOSE GRAYISH-GREEN LEAVES ARE USED IN MEDICINE AND FOR SEASONING.

3. A TYPE OF ELM TREE HAVING A STICKY INNER BARK USED AS A DEMULCENT.

4. A BIENNIAL PLANT IN THE PARSLEY FAMILY, WIDELY CULTIVATED AS AN ANNUAL FOR ITS EDIBLE TAPERING, ELONGATED, FLESHY ORANGE ROOT.

5. HIGHLY ABSORBENT, BLACK, POROUS CARBON OBTAINED BY HEATING GRANULATED CHARCOAL TO EXHAUST CONTAINED GASES, RESULTING IN A HIGHLY POROUS FORM WITH A VERY LARGE SURFACE AREA.

6. ANY OF VARIOUS HAIRY PERENNIAL EURASIAN HERBS HAVING VARIOUSLY COLORED FLOWERS LONG USED IN HERBAL MEDICINE.

9. A TROPICAL PLANT OF THE BANANA FAMILY. ITS FRUIT, EATEN COOKED IS A STAPLE FOOD IN TROPICAL REGIONS.

15. A SOUTH AMERICAN PLANT, SOLANUM TUBEROSUM, WIDELY CULTIVATED FOR ITS STARCHY EDIBLE TUBERS.

17. AN ONIONLIKE PLANT, ALLIUM SATIVUM, HAVING A BULB THAT BREAKS UP INTO SEPARABLE CLOVES WITH A STRONG DISTINCTIVE ODOR AND FLAVOR USED IN COOKERY AND MEDICINE.

CROSSWORD PUZZLE 3: ANSWERS FOUND ON PAGE 36

RAINBOW OF HEALTH 1

SEE HOW MANY FOODS YOU CAN IDENTIFY FROM THE RAINBOW

"NEVERTHELESS HE LEFT NOT HIMSELF WITHOUT WITNESS, IN THAT HE DID GOOD, AND GAVE US RAIN FROM HEAVEN, AND FRUITFUL SEASONS, FILLING OUR HEARTS WITH FOOD AND GLADNESS."

~ ACTS 14:17

RED FOODS: LYCOPENE

TREES:

PLANTS:

HERBS:

ORANGE FOODS: BETA-CAROTENE

TREES:

PLANTS:

HERBS:

YELLOW FOODS: VITAMIN C

TREES:

PLANTS:

HERBS:

GREEN FOODS: LUTEIN

TREES:

PLANTS:

HERBS:

RAINBOW FOODS: AVAILABLE ANSWERS FOUND ON PAGE 33

"FINDING HEALTH IS KEY IN THE WORD OF GOD"

SEEK AND FIND YOUR WAY THROUGH THE MAZE BELOW

Start

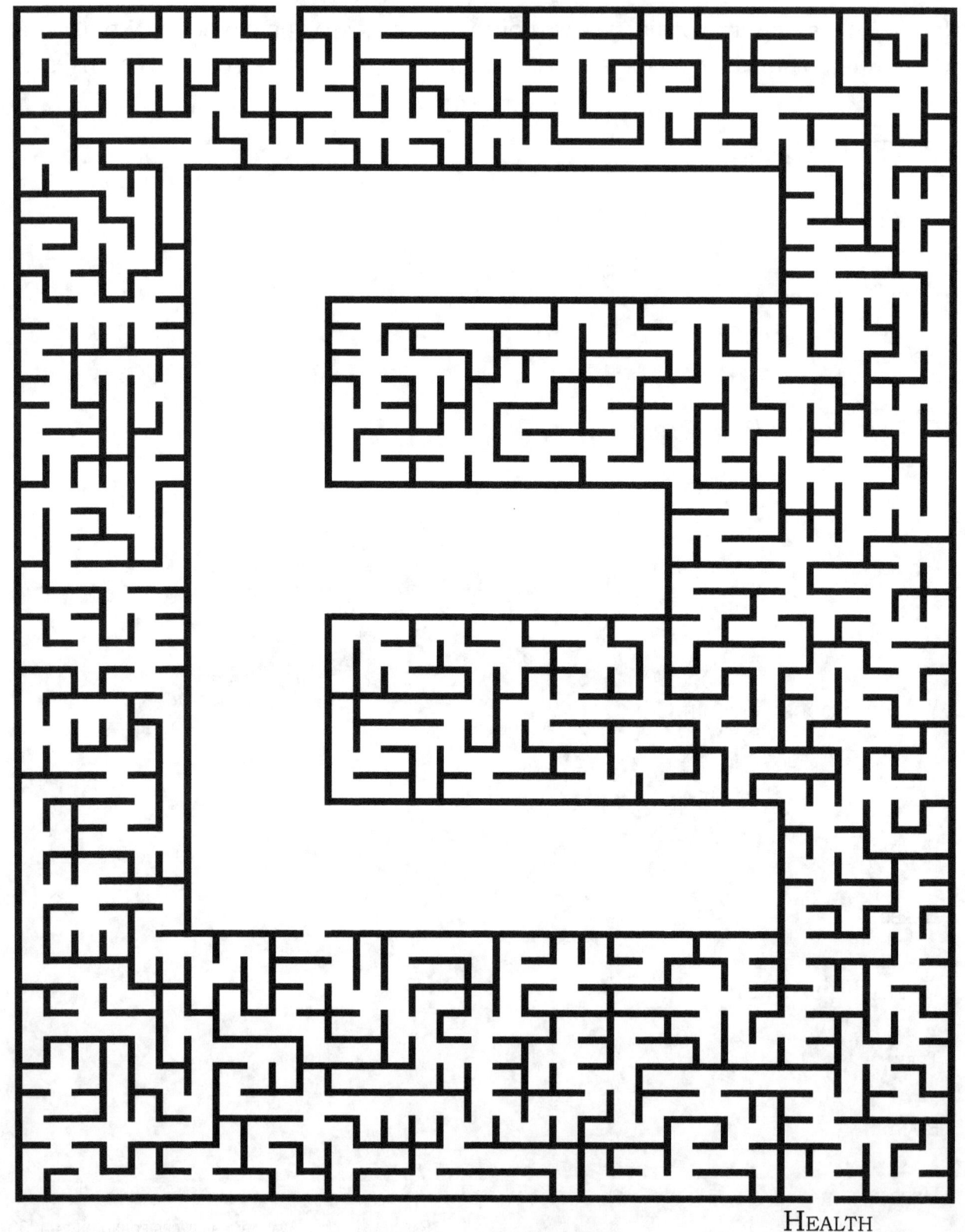

Health

POULTICES

FIND THESE WORDS IN THE FOREST OF LETTERS

```
P H J G E Y V U O G A T J F R E H R I C E V B V L
S O U G X M C N L N I H T P R Y N Y W F S E C Q I
L A G A R L I C K L C A R R O T V S Y L G P Z P C
I T A I S J K D N N Z B B X B J T F G A R N A O B
P M I M P C O M M Q F P C O M F R E Y X R O C I B
P E S U H L T Y E F K A K Z F F I G A S H R B H P
E A R J E U A I R M O P D A G P D B Q E Q H O R G
R L Q J K M Y N H P M R G E I X O Z O E V C Y W I
Y K F F M P U T T S P K Q T N U P T G D Y J U P N
E C Q L A H L X P A A P T O G H J A A P O S P I I
L C N D W I G N V B I L T F E H B P I T J M O F I
M N X Z J F B W O S A N T U R B O O N I O N U R U
A Q G V J R T R C N K V S U A T I P E L Z M L Y C
T V L I E D M S L N C X K C W O O P S I M S T P B
G N N E H V S N A T C W I T C H H A Z E L K I H K
E S A G E J X I Y M A F C H A R C O A L B T C J I
B W B O U L K U S N F S B I X V C Y U U F G E D Q
```

POULTICE	CABBAGE	GARLIC	POTATO
CARROT	COMFREY	FIG	FLAXSEED
GINGER	HOPS	OATMEAL	ONION
PLANTAIN	RICE	SAGE	SALT
SLIPPERY ELM	WITCH HAZEL	YARROW	CHARCOAL
CLAY	TOFU		

WORD SEARCH 3: ANSWERS FOUND ON PAGE 37

SEE HOW MANY WORDS
YOU CAN MAKE OUT OF

HEALING

"But unto you that fear my name shall the Sun of righteousness arise with healing in his wings; and ye shall go forth, and grow up as calves of the stall."
~ Malachi 4:2

_____

_____

_____

_____   _____

_____   _____

_____   _____

_____   _____

RAINBOW OF HEALTH 2

SEE HOW MANY FOODS YOU CAN IDENTIFY FROM THE RAINBOW

"BUT THE FRUIT OF THE SPIRIT IS LOVE, JOY, PEACE, LONGSUFFERING, GENTLENESS, GOODNESS, FAITH, MEEKNESS, TEMPERANCE: AGAINST SUCH THERE IS NO LAW."
~ GALATIANS 5:22, 23

BLUE FOODS: ANTHOCYANINS

TREES:

PLANTS:

HERBS:

WHITE FOODS: ALLICIN

TREES:

PLANTS:

HERBS:

PURPLE FOODS:

TREES:

PLANTS:

HERBS:

RAINBOW FOODS: ANSWERS FOUND ON PAGE 33

CONCEPTS ON HEALTH: BASIC PRINCIPLES 2
MATCH THE WORDS TO THEIR DEFINITIONS

1. POTATOES
   (ROOT VEGETABLES)

2. VEGETABLES

3. FRUITS

4. BREAD

5. CEREALS

6. RICE

7. WHEAT

8. SUGAR

9. NUTS

___ CONTAINS: VITAMIN A, VITAMIN C, IRON (WHEN DRIED), SUGAR. ESSENTIAL FOR A BALANCED DIET AND CAN BE EATEN AS OFTEN AS YOU LIKE. THE SWEETER THESE ARE, THE MORE CALORIES IT IS LIKELY TO CONTAIN.

___ CONTAINS: CARBOHYDRATE, VITAMIN C. THIS VEGETABLE CAN BE ONE OF THE BEST SOURCES OF CARBOHYDRATE AVAILABLE AND CAN ADD "BULK" TO A FITNESS DIET. GRILLING AND BAKING ARE THE BEST METHODS OF COOKING AS THIS KEEPS IN ALL THE NUTRIENTS AND THE TASTE OF THE FOOD.

___ CONTAINS: CARBOHYDRATE. USED TO SWEETEN FOODS TO MAKE THEM MORE PALATABLE. IT IS NOT STRICTLY NEEDED NUTRITIONALLY AND IS BETTER CUT RIGHT DOWN TO A MINIMUM.

___ CONTAINS: CARBOHYDRATE, FIBER, VITAMIN B, IRON. ONE OF THE BEST FIBER PROVIDERS. WHOLEMEAL AND BRAN-ENRICHED, PROVIDE THE BEST FIBER AND ARE A WORTHWHILE ADDITIVE TO YOUR DIET.

___ CONTAIN: PROTEIN, FIBER, VITAMIN A (CARROTS), FOLIC ACID (GREENS), VITAMIN E, CALCIUM (GREENS/PULSES), IRON (GREENS). ALTHOUGH MOST CONTAIN HIGH AMOUNTS OF WATER, THEY DO CONTAIN LARGE QUANTITIES OF NUTRIENTS.

___ CONTAINS: PROTEIN, POLYUNSATURATED FATS. CAN BE USED ON THEIR OWN OR AS AN INGREDIENT TO OTHER FOODS. THEY PROVIDE A VERY HIGH SOURCE OF ENERGY BUT MAY ALSO BE HIGH IN CALORIES. TRY TO AVOID SALTED AND GO INSTEAD FOR BRAZIL, WALL AND HAZEL VARIETIES WHICH ALL INCLUDE EXTRA NUTRIENTS.

___ CONTAIN: PROTEIN, POLYUNSATURATED FATS, CARBOHYDRATE, VITAMIN E, IRON. COMMONLY REFERRED TO AS "BREAKFAST" FOODS: IT CAN CONTAIN HIGH FIBER LEVELS AND CAN BE EATEN ANYTIME AS A MEAL. WHEAT BASED VARIANTS SUCH AS SHREDDED WHEAT AND WHEAT BISCUITS ARE HIGH IN FIBER AND PROTEIN. PORRIDGE AND OTHER OAT BASED ALTERNATIVES ALSO CONTAIN FEW CALORIES.

___ CONTAINS: FIBER. AGAIN, FIBER ONE OF ITS PROPERTIES. ALWAYS BOIL TO HELP RETAIN ITS NUTRIENTS. NEVER FRY AS THIS WILL INCREASE ITS CALORIE VALUE GREATLY.

___ CONTAINS: PROTEIN (SMALL AMOUNTS), FIBER. CAN BE USED IN FOOD PREPARATION BUT ALSO FOUND IN CEREALS AND FOOD BARS. ONE OF THE BEST SOURCES OF FIBER, IT IS AN ESSENTIAL INGREDIENT TO ANY DIET.

DEFINITIONS: ANSWERS FOUND ON PAGE 35

"FINDING HEALTH IS KEY IN THE WORD OF GOD"

SEEK AND FIND YOUR WAY THROUGH THE MAZE BELOW

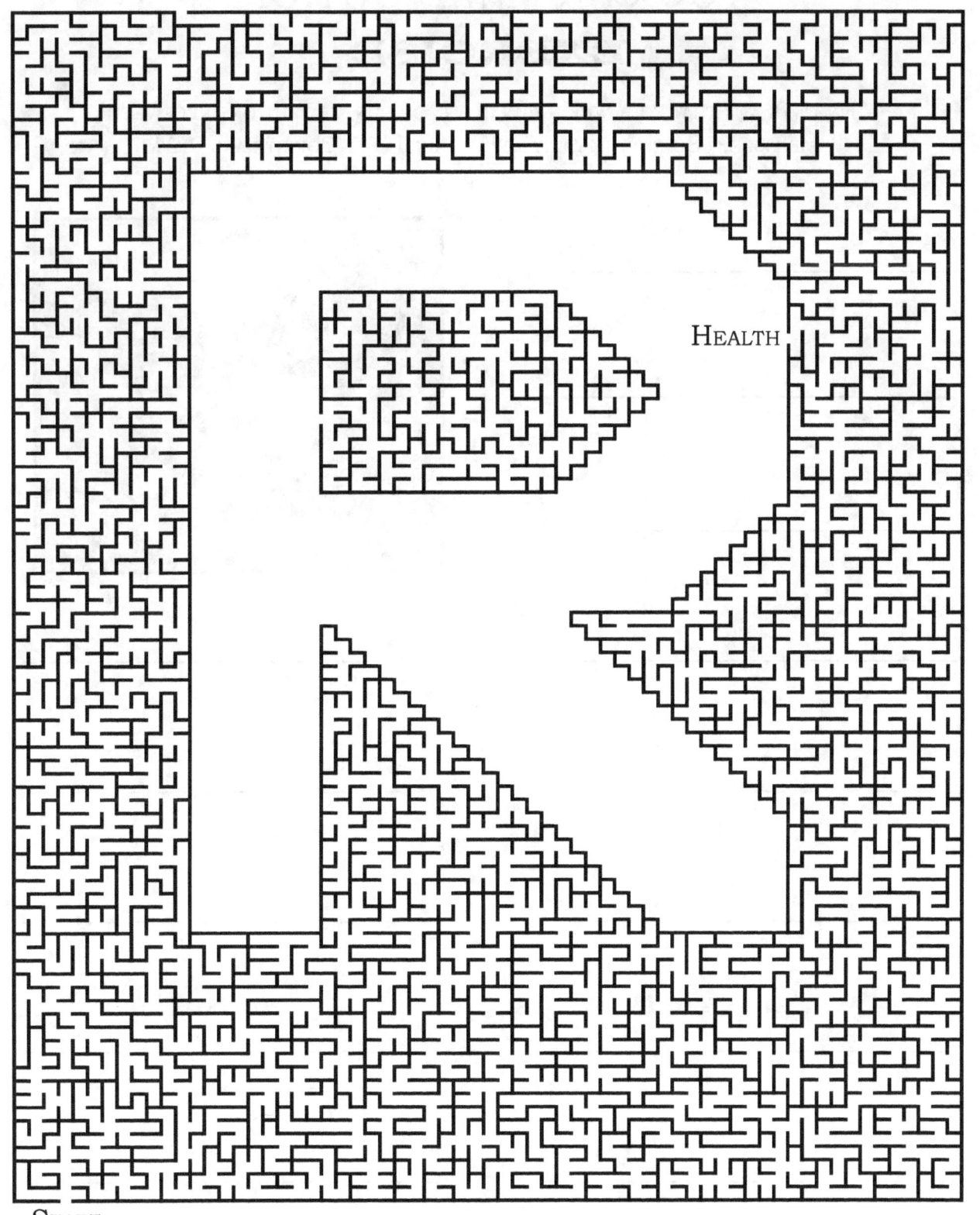

HEALTH

START

SEE HOW MANY WORDS
YOU CAN MAKE OUT OF
EXERCISE

"KNOW YE NOT THAT THEY WHICH RUN IN A RACE RUN ALL, BUT ONE RECEIVETH THE PRIZE? SO RUN, THAT YE MAY OBTAIN." ~ 1 CORINTHIANS 9:24

_____

_____

_____

_____   _____

_____   _____

_____   _____

_____   _____

SECRET MESSAGE 4

A	B	C	D	E	F	G	H	I	J	K	L	M	N	O	P	Q	R	S	T	U	V	W	X	Y	Z
12	22	4	17	3	14	24	16	5	18	1	11	2	21	6	10	20	7	26	13	25	8	15	23	9	19

USE THE ABOVE KEYS TO DECODE THE MESSAGE BELOW

_22_ _3_ _16_ _6_ _11_ _17_ , _16_ _12_ _10_ _10_ _9_

_5_ _26_ _13_ _16_ _3_ _2_ _12_ _21_ _15_ _16_ _6_ _2_ _24_ _6_ _17_ _4_ _6_ _7_ _7_ _3_ _4_ _13_ _26_ ;

_13_ _16_ _3_ _7_ _3_ _14_ _6_ _7_ _3_ _17_ _6_ _21_ _6_ _13_

_17_ _3_ _26_ _10_ _5_ _26_ _3_ _13_ _16_ _3_

_4_ _16_ _12_ _26_ _13_ _3_ _21_ _5_ _21_ _24_ _6_ _14_

_13_ _16_ _3_ _12_ _11_ _2_ _5_ _24_ _16_ _13_ _9_ .

_14_ _6_ _7_ _16_ _3_ _22_ _7_ _25_ _5_ _26_ _3_ _26_ ,

_22_ _25_ _13_ _16_ _3_ _22_ _5_ _21_ _17_ _26_ _25_ _10_ ;

_16_ _3_ _15_ _6_ _25_ _21_ _17_ _26_ , _22_ _25_ _13_

_16_ _5_ _26_ _16_ _12_ _21_ _17_ _26_

_2_ _12_ _1_ _3_ _15_ _16_ _6_ _11_ _3_ .

WHERE IS THIS TEXT FOUND? _____

SECRET MESSAGE 4: ANSWERS FOUND ON PAGE 34

27

ALL TYPES OF THERAPY
FIND THESE WORDS IN THE FOREST OF LETTERS

```
B Y E M K T Q U N K N C F V D E A Q S B A A A K W
F L U X I O N O Y F I B A G V R N K L U L E N W S
V K M Q Y G I G H N N W L I I E T D X I J A T L D
Z P D Q S T F R O J M N T D K F I O U P O H I A X
H V C C E P G T D R J A E X F R S V R X U L P L Z
S H W L T F Z D A G I V L I S I P E X N N D Y T H
T T P G S Q Q F T L I K Y Y E G A B S Z L W R E Y
G E I Z O Z K X O S O F B T D E S N A W D X E R J
D W C M R M Z P L A W Y N U A R M B O O F F T N U
I B X M U P S U W V T A S M T A O H D D K B I A N
V D U Q I L V P X V S T Q H I N D R I U Y I C T R
M I O X U E A Q N S L G S A V T I S G H F N T I D
Q W S I R R F N E L V S J B E E C K E U K M E V M
H V K N B M P R T M P O B D E R I V A T I V E E I
Q T I I F N P R E D I U R E S I S D Z I H E C B B
M E P L P E L F K I D I A P H O R E S I S V H M Y
D P C N D Y T M E L I M I N A T I V E E W E N E S
```

TONIC	STIMULANT	SEDATIVE
ANTISPASMODIC	DEPRESSANT	ANODYNE
SPOLIATIVE	DIAPHORESIS	DIURESIS
ELIMINATIVE	DEPLETION	DERIVATIVE
FLUXION	ANTIPYRETIC	REFRIGERANT
REVULSIVE	ALTERNATIVE	

WORD SEARCH 4: ANSWERS FOUND ON PAGE 37

COLORING ACTIVITY

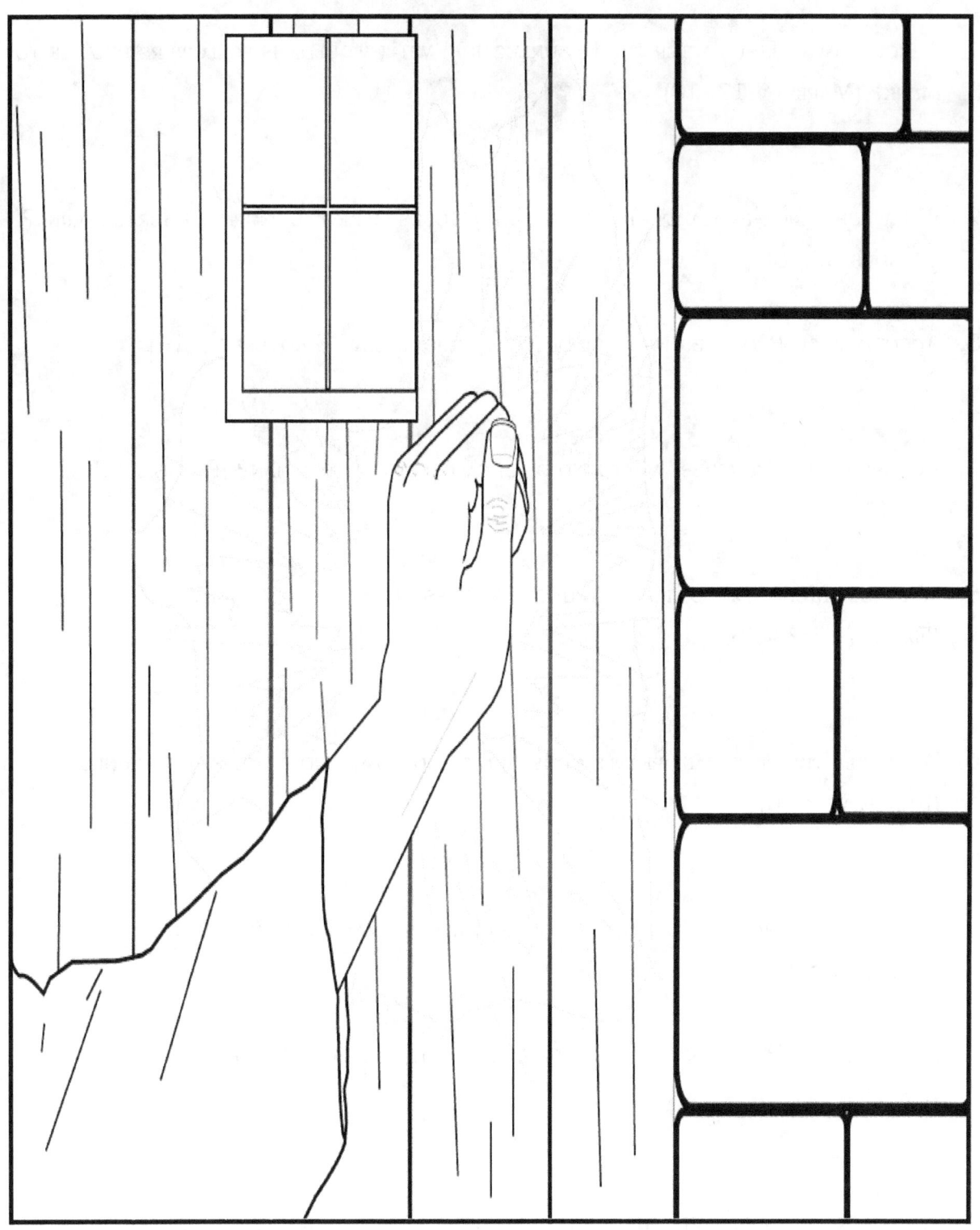

THE KNOCK

BIBLE TRIVIA 3: FOOD FOR THOUGHT

1. ACCORDING TO JESUS AFTER THE RESURRECTION, WHAT WOULD HIS FOLLOWERS BE ABLE TO DRINK? (MARK 16:17, 18)

2. WHAT SUBSTANCE-PROBABLY VERY BITTER-DID MOSES MAKE THE PEOPLE OF ISRAEL DRINK? (EXODUS 30:20)

3. ACCORDING TO PROVERBS, WHAT KIND OF WATER IS SWEET? (PROVERBS 9:17)

4. ACCORDING TO PROVERBS, WHAT KIND OF BREAD IS SWEET TO A MAN? (PROVERBS 20:17)

5. WHAT DID MOSES DO TO MAKE THE BITTER WATERS OF MARAH DRINKABLE? (EXODUS 15:23-25)

6. WHO TOLD THE REPENTANT PEOPLE OF ISRAEL TO GO HOME AND ENJOY SWEET DRINKS? (NEHEMIAH 8:10)

7. IN REVELATION, WHAT FALLS ON THE EARTH'S WATERS TO MAKE THEM BITTER? (REVELATION 8:10)

8. ACCORDING TO PROVERBS, WHAT SORT OF PERSON THINKS EVEN BITTER THINGS ARE SWEET? (PROVERBS 27:7)

9. ACCORDING TO JEREMIAH, WHAT KIND OF GRAPE SETS THE CHILDREN'S TEETH ON EDGE? (JEREMIAH 31:29)

BIBLE TRIVIA 3: ANSWERS FOUND ON PAGE 32

"FINDING HEALTH IS KEY IN THE WORD OF GOD"

SEEK AND FIND YOUR WAY THROUGH THE MAZE BELOW

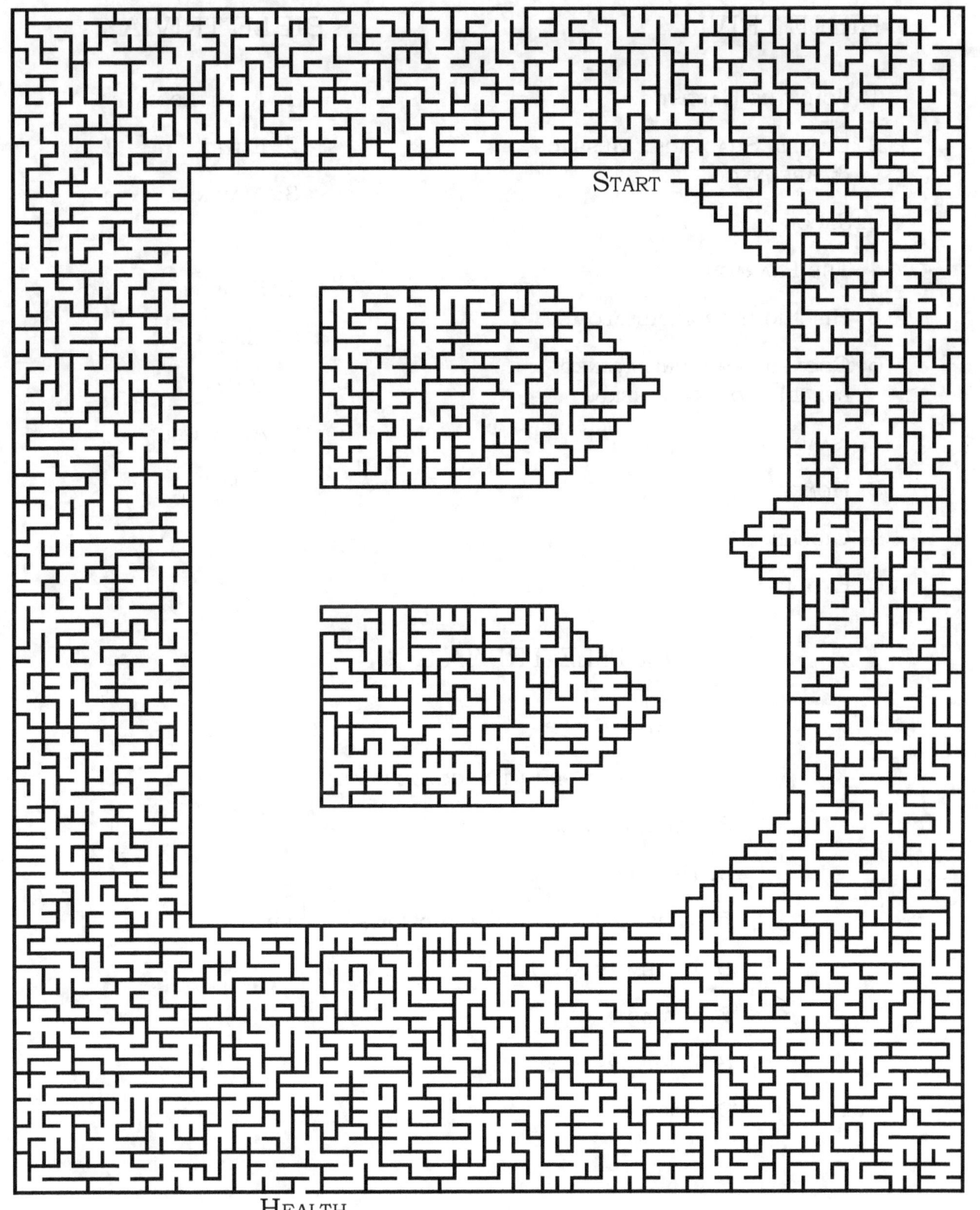

START

HEALTH

ANSWER PAGES

BIBLE TRIVIA 1

1. JOHN THE BAPTIST

2. DANIEL, SHADRACH, MESHACH, & ABEDNEGO

3. JACOB

4. THE PHARAOH

5. HIS FLIGHT FROM ABSALOM

6. COOKED LAMB, UNLEAVENED BREAD, AND BITTER HERBS

7. ISAAC

8. HONEY

9. GIDEON

10. EXODUS

BIBLE TRIVIA 2

1. A FATTED CALF

2. EGYPT

3. ALMONDS

4. AMOS

5. SAMSON

6. MANNA

7. BREAD

8. AN ANGEL

9. ELIJAH

BIBLE TRIVIA 3

1. POISON

2. GOLD DUST FROM THE GOLDEN CALF

3. STOLEN WATER

4. BREAD OF DECEIT

5. THREW A PIECE OF WOOD INTO THE WATER

6. NEHEMIAH AND EZRA

7. A STAR

8. A HUNGRY PERSON

9. SOUR

SECRET MESSAGE 1

THERE IS THAT SPEAKETH LIKE THE PIERCINGS OF A SWORD: BUT THE TONGUE OF THE WISE IS HEALTH.

PROVERBS 12:18

SECRET MESSAGE 2

AND ISAIAH SAID, TAKE A LUMP OF FIGS. AND THEY TOOK AND LAID IT ON THE BOIL, AND HE RECOVERED.

2 KINGS 20:7

SECRET MESSAGE 3

EXODUS 15:26

DEUTERONOMY 7:15

PSALM 91:16

JEREMIAH 30:17

ISAIAH 53:4-5

SECRET MESSAGE 4

BEHOLD, HAPPY IS THE MAN WHOM GOD CORRECTS; THEREFORE DO NOT DESPISE THE CHASTENING OF THE ALMIGHTY. FOR HE BRUISES, BUT HE BINDS UP; HE WOUNDS, BUT HIS HANDS MAKE WHOLE.

JOB 5:17, 18

RAINBOW HEALTH
HERE ARE A FEW, DID YOU FIND ANYMORE?

PART 1

RED FOODS: LYCOPENES
TREES: CHERRIES, APPLES, CRANBERRIES, PAPAYA, POMEGRANATE
PLANTS: TOMATOES, STRAWBERRIES, WATERMELON, RASPBERRIES
HERBS: BEETS, RHUBARB, RADISHES

ORANGE FOODS: BETA-CAROTENE
TREES: ORANGES, GRAPEFRUIT, PEACHES
PLANTS: PUMPKIN, SQUASH
HERBS: CARROTS, SWEET POTATOES, YAMS

YELLOW FOODS: VITAMIN C
TREES: LEMONS, PINEAPPLES, BANANAS, APRICOTS
PLANTS: CORN, SQUASH, WHEAT, CANTALOUPE
HERBS: RUTABAGAS

GREEN FOODS: LUTEIN
TREES: AVOCADOS, OLIVES, PEARS, LIME
PLANTS: CUCUMBERS, PEAS, GREEN BEANS, ZUCCHINI
HERBS: BROCCOLI, ASPARAGUS, GREENS, SPINACH, BRUSSELS SPROUTS, KALE, CELERY, GREEN ONIONS

PART 2

BLUE FOODS: ANTHOCYANINS
PLANTS: BLUEBERRIES

WHITE FOODS: ALLICIN
TREES: COCONUT, DATES, PEARS, NUTS
PLANTS: WHITE BEANS, OATS
HERBS: ONIONS, CAULIFLOWER, GARLIC, HORSERADISH, POTATOES, TURNIPS, MUSHROOMS, PARSNIPS, SHALLOTS, GINGER

PURPLE FOODS:
TREES: PLUMBS, PRUNES, FIGS
PLANTS: GRAPES, BLACKBERRIES, ELDERBERRIES
HERBS: BEETS, EGGPLANTS, CABBAGE

CONCEPTS ON HEALTH: BASIC PRINCIPLES 1

1. REGULARITY IN MEALS

$\underline{3}$ ONLY PUT A SMALL AMOUNT IN YOUR MOUTH AT A TIME. YOU WILL CHEW AND SALIVATE IT BETTER, AND TEND TO EAT LESS AT THAT MEAL.

2. MODERATION

$\underline{9}$ SAY NO TO GRAVIES, VEGETABLE LOAVES, GLUTEN FOODS, AND ALL THE REST. KEEP YOUR MEAL SIMPLE.

3. TAKE SMALL BITES

$\underline{12}$ IT IS VERY RICH SOURCE OF IRON. IT IS ALSO A SOURCE OF CHOLINE AND INOSITOL, THE TWO B VITAMINS USED IN THE LARGEST QUANTITIES.

4. RELAX AND EAT SLOWLY

$\underline{11}$ IF YOU ATE OATMEAL THIS MORNING, TRY RYE OR WHEAT TOMORROW.

5. NOT TOO MANY THINGS PER MEAL

$\underline{5}$ THREE OR FOUR ITEMS (PLUS A LITTLE SALT, CORRECT OILS, ETC.) ARE ALL YOU NEED.

6. NO DRINKING

$\underline{10}$ SUCH AS VINEGAR, MONOSODIUM GLUTAMATE, ETC., WHICH ONLY UPSET YOUR STOMACH AND SLOW DIGESTION.

7. SEA VEGETABLE

$\underline{6}$ ASIDE FROM FRESH, RAW JUICES OR THE GREEN DRINK, DRINK ALL YOUR LIQUIDS (WATER) BETWEEN MEALS NOT WITH YOUR MEALS.

8. MIXED UP

$\underline{7}$ NOVA SCOTIA DULSE AND NORWEGIAN KELP (TWO TYPES OF SEAWEED) ARE THE ONLY RICH SOURCE OF TRACE MINERALS.

9. AVOID COMPLICATED MIXTURES

$\underline{8}$ REST BEFORE THE MEAL AND WALK AROUND AFTER IT, NOT VICE VERSA.

10. AVOID PECULIAR ADDITIVES

$\underline{4}$ IF YOU ARE TOO RUSHED TO EAT, THEN DO NOT EAT. DO NOT BE HURRIED, ANXIOUS, WORRIED, FATIGUED OR ANGRY.

11. VARY YOUR MEALS

$\underline{1}$ DO NOT EAT THEM EARLY OR LATE, BUT MAINTAIN A REGULAR SCHEDULE. YOUR STOMACH IS USED TO EATING AT CERTAIN TIMES EACH DAY.

12. BLACK STRAP MOLASSES

$\underline{2}$ ONLY EAT AS MUCH AS YOU NEED. NEVER OVEREAT. ONLY EAT TO SATISFY HUNGER, AND THEN STOP.

CONCEPTS ON HEALTH: BASIC PRINCIPLES 2

1. POTATOES
   (ROOT VEGETABLES)

   _3_   CONTAINS: VITAMIN A, VITAMIN C, IRON (WHEN DRIED), SUGAR. ESSENTIAL FOR A BALANCED DIET AND CAN BE EATEN AS OFTEN AS YOU LIKE. THE SWEETER, THE MORE CALORIES IT CONTAINS.

2. VEGETABLES

   _1_   CONTAINS: CARBOHYDRATE, VITAMIN C. THIS VEGETABLE CAN BE ONE OF THE BEST SOURCES OF CARBOHYDRATES AVAILABLE AND CAN ADD 'BULK' TO A FITNESS DIET.

3. FRUITS

   _8_   CONTAINS: CARBOHYDRATE. USED TO SWEETEN FOODS TO MAKE THEM MORE PALATABLE, BUT IT IS NOT STRICTLY NEEDED NUTRITIONALLY.

4. BREAD

   _4_   CONTAINS: CARBOHYDRATE, FIBRE, VITAMIN B, IRON. ONE OF THE BEST FIBRE PROVIDERS. WHOLEMEAL AND BRAN-ENRICHED, PROVIDE THE BEST FIBRE AND ARE A WORTHWHILE ADDITIVE TO YOUR DIET.

5. CEREALS

   _2_   CONTAIN: PROTEIN, FIBER, VITAMIN A (CARROTS), FOLIC ACID (GREENS), VITAMIN E, CALCIUM (GREENS/PULSES), IRON (GREENS). ALTHOUGH IT CONTAINS HIGH AMOUNTS OF WATER, THEY DO CONTAIN LARGE QUANTITIES OF NUTRIENTS.

6. RICE

   _9_   CONTAINS: PROTEIN, POLYUNSATURATED FATS. THEY PROVIDE A VERY HIGH SOURCE OF ENERGY BUT MAY ALSO BE HIGH IN CALORIES. AVOID SALTED AND GO FOR BRAZIL, WALL AND HAZEL VARIETIES WHICH ALL INCLUDE EXTRA NUTRIENTS.

7. WHEAT

   _5_   CONTAINS: PROTEIN, POLYUNSATURATED FATS, CARBOHYDRATE, VITAMIN E, IRON. WHEAT BASED VARIANTS SUCH AS SHREDDED WHEAT AND WHEAT BISCUITS ARE HIGH IN FIBRE AND PROTEIN. PORRIDGE AND OTHER OAT BASED ALTERNATIVES ALSO CONTAIN FEW CALORIES.

8. SUGAR

   _6_   CONTAINS: FIBRE. ALWAYS BOIL TO HELP RETAIN ITS NUTRIENTS. NEVER FRY AS THIS WILL INCREASE ITS CALORIE VALUE GREATLY.

9. NUTS

   _7_   CONTAINS: PROTEIN (SMALL AMOUNTS), FIBRE. CAN BE USED IN FOOD PREPARATION BUT ALSO FOUND IN CEREALS AND FOOD BARS. ONE OF THE BEST SOURCES OF FIBRE, IT IS AN ESSENTIAL INGREDIENT TO ANY DIET.

CROSSWORD PUZZLE 1

CROSSWORD PUZZLE 2

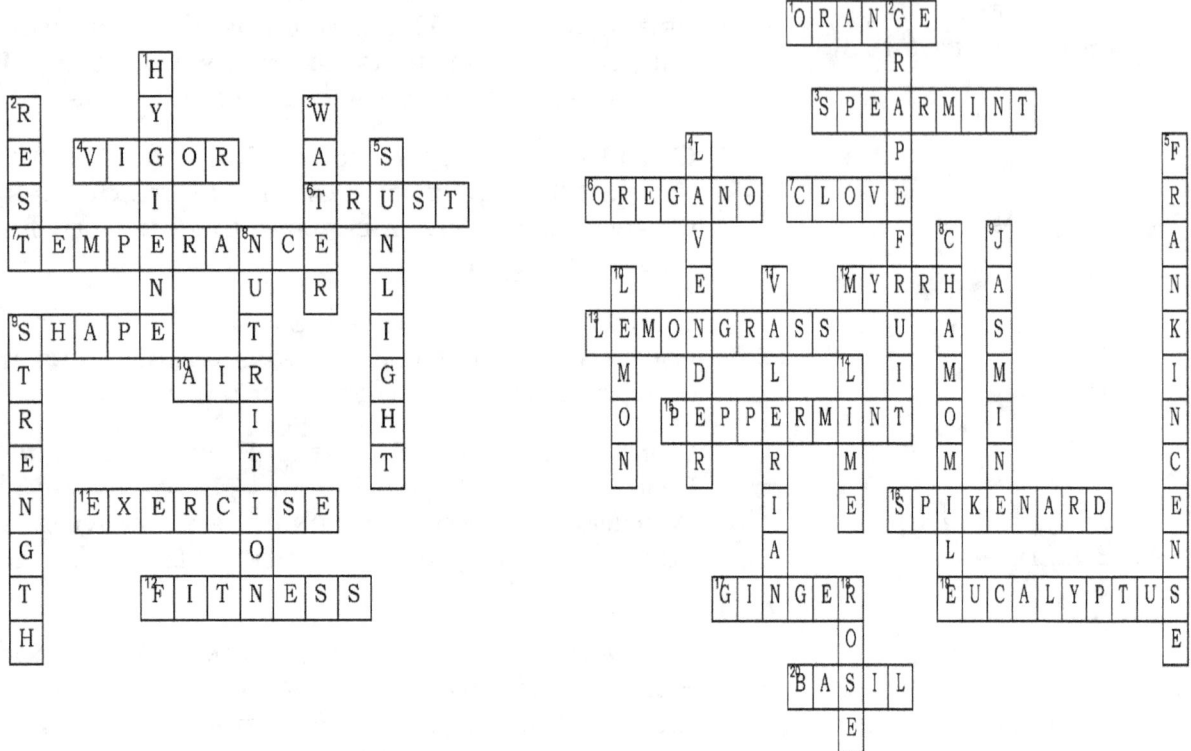

CROSSWORD PUZZLE 3

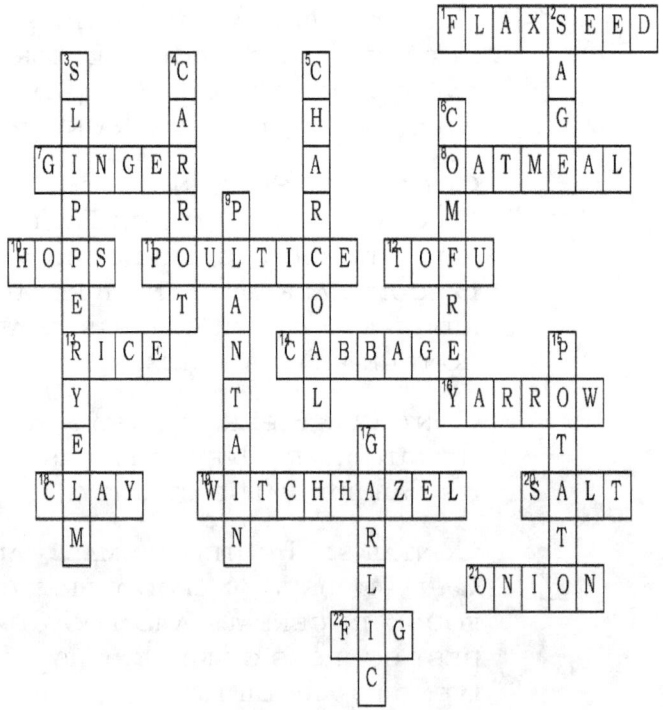

Word Search 1

```
U O Z Y G E E V V U S U B P V C A D V P V Y L N D
D S R O C N U Z F O R W M E X E R C I S E P U Y H
I F H I E M V G B S R O G S A N E I A F E R N E A
S N X I Z U E A I M W T X R O N B R U L T G B E O
A I G W J L B C W I I W I C L T T V W Y P H O H
C Y D P E W A T E R Y W T E J L P Y B U M K H Y P
H T F N O K T H E R K I Z W W W Y I M M I B X F S
P Q J C E H J T I R L C G Y E I C T R S C V L H
J E W P J E B A E T I V P K C Q V S R K O F E C A
M S G E P Q H W U X B Q Y P W N C W T M Y Z L T P
M N U J O O S N M V I G O R I W T A I R W S S P E
E P G N B E K A W X M Y Y W U U K G E V E U R B P
C K Q W L U F X R T E M P E R A N C E S R N Z G Q
D X H Q R I X R C E E A E O S I K G X T G N G K C
X B S P M K G A V T S T F I T N E S S M J O D T S
J B L F L M N H V W A T N C V Z T A X G S F X U H
F O P C J O B I T A Z E V F F E D I Q N X D C S V
```

Word Search 2

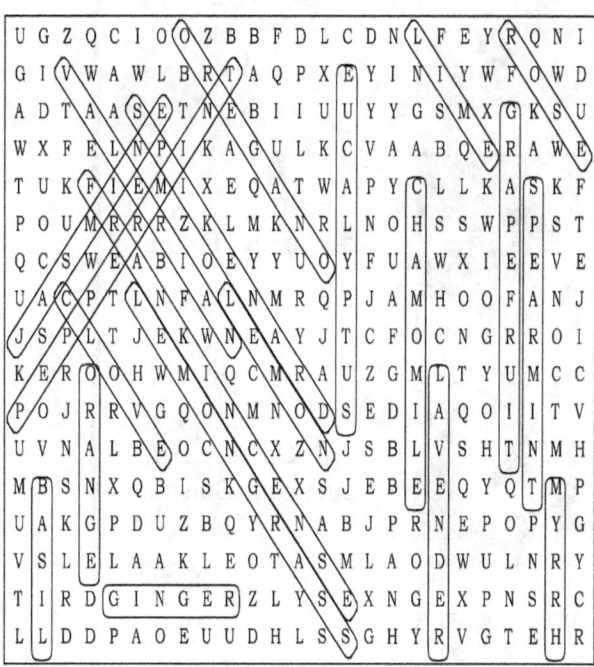

Word Search 3

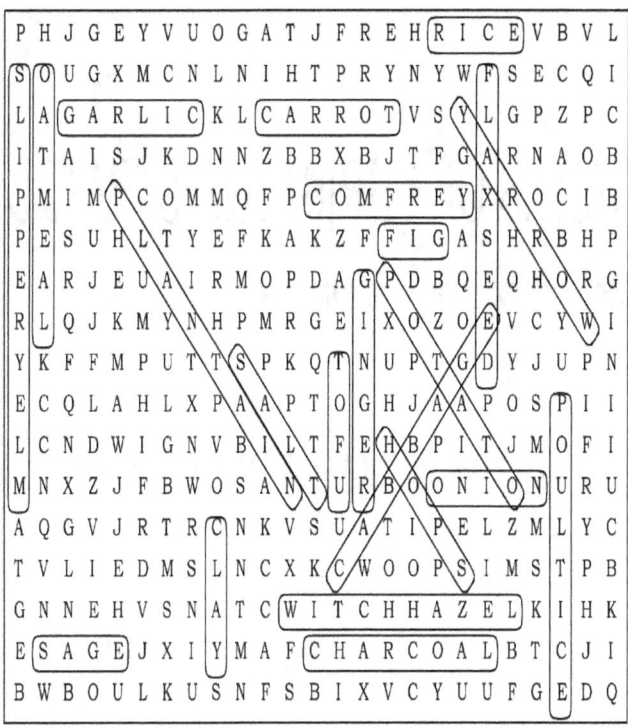

Word Search 4

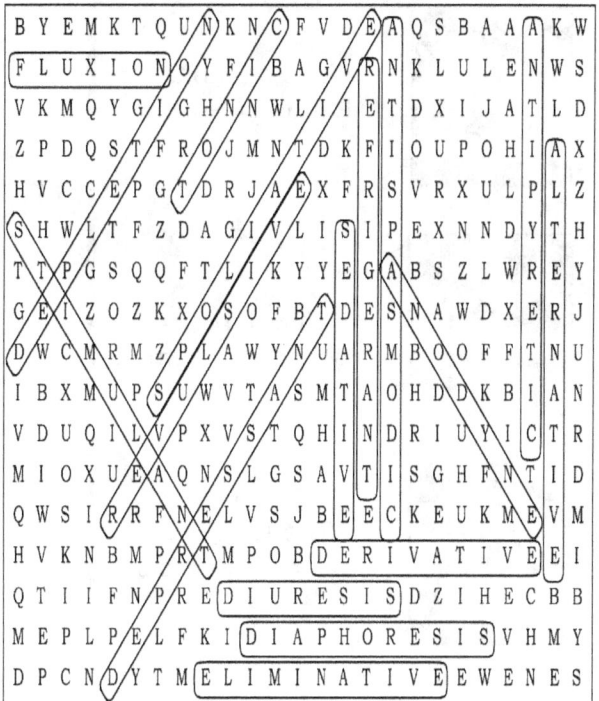

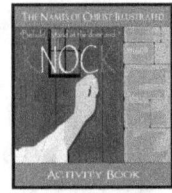

THE NOC ILLUSTRATED
ACTIVITY BOOK

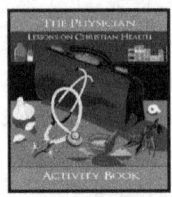

THE PHYSICIAN:
CHRISTIAN HEALTH

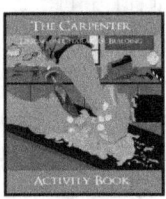

THE CARPENTER:
CHARACTER BUILDING

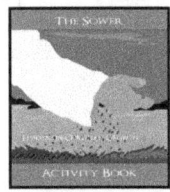

THE SOWER:
CHRISTIAN GROWTH

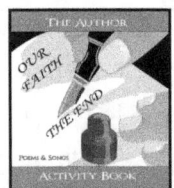

THE AUTHOR:
POEMS & SONGS

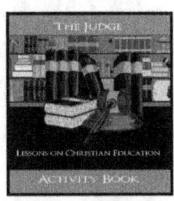

THE JUDGE:
CHRISTIAN EDUCATION

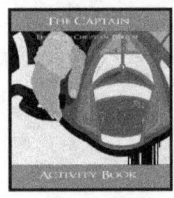

THE CAPTAIN:
CHRISTIAN PURPOSE

"PORTRAITS OF THE SAVIOUR'S
DESIRE TO ENTER HEARTS."

THIS BOOK:

THE PHYSICIAN

LESSONS ON CHRISTIAN HEALTH

THE NAMES OF CHRIST ILLUSTRATED

PLEASE VISIT US ONLINE TO VIEW
MORE GREAT TITLES AT:

WWW.THENOCILLUSTRATED.COM

www.ingramcontent.com/pod-product-compliance
Lightning Source LLC
Chambersburg PA
CBHW081239170526
45165CB00009B/3116